Nora the Naturalist's Animals

Pond Life

FRANKLIN WATTS
LONDON • SYDNEY

Franklin Watts
First published in Great Britain in 2015 by The Watts Publishing Group

Designed and illustrated by David West

Dewey number 591.76
HB ISBN 978 1 4451 4496 2

Printed in Malaysia

Franklin Watts
An imprint of
Hachette Children's Group
Part of The Watts Publishing Group
Carmelite House
50 Victoria Embankment
London EC4Y 0DZ

An Hachette UK Company
www.hachette.co.uk

www.franklinwatts.co.uk

NORA THE NATURALIST'S ANIMALS POND LIFE
was produced for Franklin Watts by
David West Children's Books, 6 Princeton Court, 55 Felsham Road, London SW15 1AZ

Nora the Naturalist says:
I will tell you something
more about the animal.

Learn what this
animal eats.

Where in the
world is the
animal found?

Its size is revealed!

What animal group
is it – mammal, bird,
reptile, amphibian,
insect, or something
else?

Interesting facts.

Contents

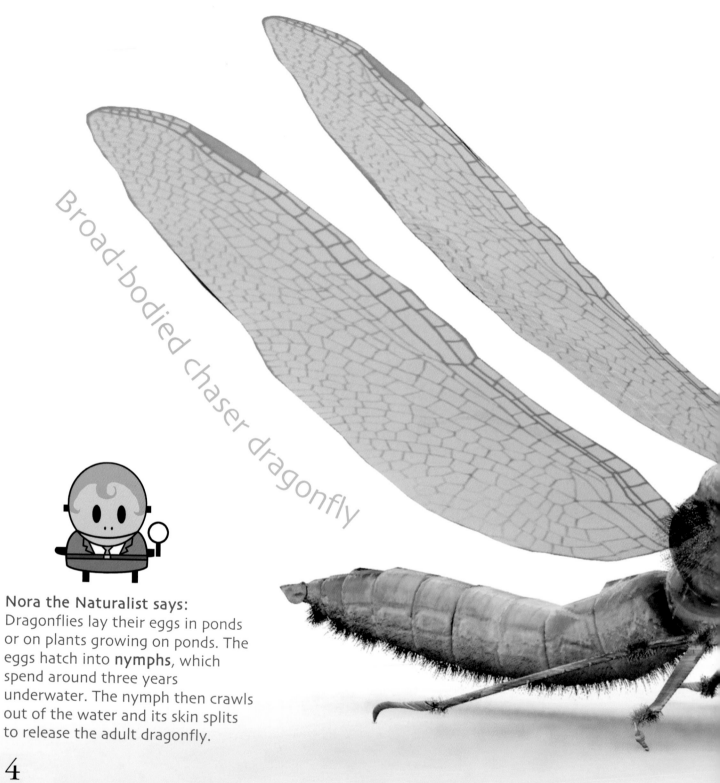

Broad-bodied chaser dragonfly

Nora the Naturalist says:
Dragonflies lay their eggs in ponds or on plants growing on ponds. The eggs hatch into **nymphs**, which spend around three years underwater. The nymph then crawls out of the water and its skin splits to release the adult dragonfly.

Dragonflies eat other insects and even small fish when they are nymphs.

Dragonflies can be found in wetlands all over the world, except in the polar regions.

The average wingspan of this dragonfly is 70 millimetres.

Dragonflies are insects. They are not members of the true fly family.

Large dragonflies have a maximum speed of 10–15 metres per second.

Dragonflies

Dragonflies are one of the fastest insect fliers. They hunt other insects, such as mosquitos and flies. They spend most of their life as nymphs living underwater.

Nora the Naturalist says:
Pond skaters are also known as water striders, water bugs, magic bugs, skimmers, water scooters, water skaters, water skeeters, water skimmers and water skippers.

Pond skater

Pond Skaters

Pond skaters can be seen on ponds, scooting across the surface. Microscopic hairs on their legs trap air bubbles that allow them to float on the water's surface. They have wings so they can fly away from water to **hibernate** during the winter.

Pond skaters feed on insects that fall into the water.

Pond skaters are found in ponds around the world in **temperate** or **tropical** climates.

Pond skaters measure about 20 millimetres long.

Pond skaters are members of the true bugs family of insects.

Pond skaters are very agile on the surface of the water and can jump to evade **predators**.

Mosquitos

Mosquitos are found in warm and humid places where there is standing water. They lay their eggs in or on the water. Only the female mosquito sucks blood from animals. They can pass on diseases, such as **malaria**.

Nora the Naturalist says:
In warm countries of the world they are active all year, but in cooler countries they hibernate in winter. Arctic mosquitos may live for only a few weeks until their pools of water freeze over.

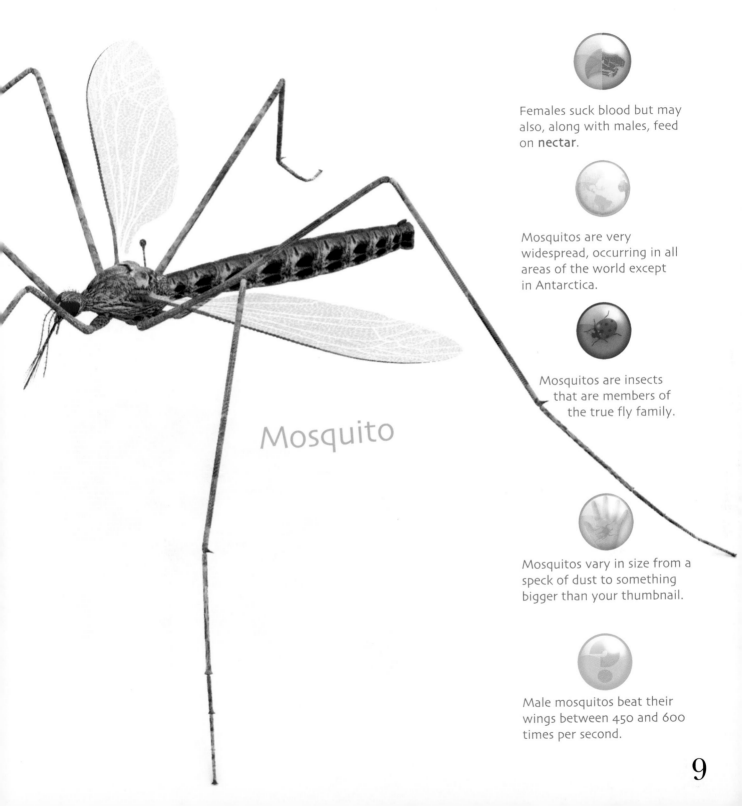

Mosquito

Females suck blood but may also, along with males, feed on **nectar**.

Mosquitos are very widespread, occurring in all areas of the world except in Antarctica.

Mosquitos are insects that are members of the true fly family.

Mosquitos vary in size from a speck of dust to something bigger than your thumbnail.

Male mosquitos beat their wings between 450 and 600 times per second.

Carp eat floating plants, algae, mosquitos, midge flies, larvae, unlucky bugs near the water's surface, tadpoles and small fish. They also sift through mud for worms, freshwater shrimps and snails.

Native to central Asia, carp are the most widely distributed freshwater fish in the world.

Carp are members of the ray-finned fish family.

Carp can grow to very large sizes but koi generally grow to around 30 centimetres.

Koi were originally bred in Japan in various colours and patterns.

Koi

10

Carp

Various types of carp have been **domesticated** and bred for food in ponds across Europe and Asia for thousands of years. They have also been bred as **ornamental** fish for pets.

Nora the Naturalist says:
Koi are a domesticated variety of common carp that have been bred for their colourful patterns.

Wild Fish

Wild ponds may contain a variety of wild fish, the most common being the stickleback. The male stickleback is a very good father.

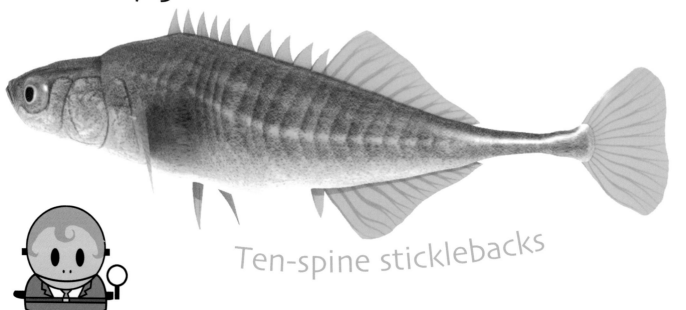

Ten-spine sticklebacks

Nora the Naturalist says: The male stickleback makes a nest from vegetation. It will guard the eggs in the nest until they hatch.

12

Sticklebacks eat worms, insect larvae and crustaceans.

Sticklebacks live in freshwater and saltwater and are common in mild northern climates around the world, including Europe, North America, Asia and Japan.

Their maximum length is about 10 centimetres but few of them grow to more than 8 centimetres.

Sticklebacks are members of the ray-finned fish family.

They are also known as burnstickle, common stickleback, European stickleback, jacksharp and tiddler.

Turtles

In some parts of the world, freshwater turtles can be found living in and around ponds. These shy animals are good swimmers. They hunt for various types of water creatures and also feed on plants.

Nora the Naturalist says:
Red-eared sliders get their name from the red patch of skin on their neck and their ability to slide off rocks into the water quickly.

14

They eat a variety of food, including fish, crayfish, tadpoles, snails, crickets, worms, water insects and many water plants.

Freshwater turtles can be found all over the world, except in the polar regions. The red-eared slider used to be found naturally only in parts of North America and Mexico.

The female red-eared slider grows to 25–33 centimetres in length.

Turtles are members of the reptile family.

Due to their popularity as pets, many red-eared sliders have escaped or been released into the wild. Because of this red-eared sliders are now found in Australia and in the UK.

Frogs

Frogs are amphibians which means they can live on land and in water. Frogs start life as tadpoles after hatching from frogspawn. Eventually they lose their tail and gills and become air-breathing frogs.

Nora the Naturalist says:
Frogs can catch flies on their long, sticky tongues.

Common frog

Favourite foods include insects, snails, slugs and worms.

Frogs are found on all the continents, except Antarctica.

Frogs are amphibians.

Adult common frogs have a body length of 6 to 9 centimetres.

Some frogs, such as the poison dart frogs, have poisonous skin.

Toads

Toads are like frogs. They lay their eggs in ponds. After changing into an adult toad they spend most of their life on land. They have warty-looking skin, which helps them blend into their surroundings.

Nora the Naturalist says:
Toads give off a poison from skin glands when they are disturbed. This stops most predators from eating them.

American toad

Their diet includes crickets, worms, ants, spiders, slugs, centipedes, moths and other small insects.

Toads are widespread and live on every continent except Antarctica.

Toads are members of the amphibian family.

The American toad is a medium-sized toad around 5–9 centimetres in length.

Some toads, like the American toad, hibernate during winter.

19

Newts

Newts hatch from eggs in a pond and go through a change from tadpole to juvenile. The juveniles leave the pond to grow into adults. Then they either return to live in the water for the rest of their lives, or live on land, returning to the water each year to lay eggs.

Nora the Naturalist says:
When the juvenile newt leaves the water and lives on land it is called an eft.

Red-spotted newt

Newts eat insects, snails, crustaceans, young amphibians, frogs' eggs and worms.

Newts are found in North America, Europe, the Middle East, Southeast Asia and Japan.

Newts are amphibians that are members of the salamander family.

Many newts produce poisons from their skin as a defence against predators.

The red-spotted newt may grow to 12.5 centimetres in length.

Herons prey on fish, frogs and other small water animals.

Herons can be found on every continent in the world except Antarctica.

Herons are members of the bird family.

Herons vary in size from 44–152 centimetres or more in length.

Herons have long legs so that they can wade in water without getting their feathers wet.

Grey heron

Purple heron

22

Herons

Ponds around the world may get occasional visits from a heron. These patient birds hunt for fish and other small water animals in shallow water.

Green heron

Little blue heron

Nora the Naturalist says:
Some species of heron, such as the little egret and grey heron, have been seen using bait, such as bits of bread, in order to attract **prey**.

23

Glossary

domesticated
Changed by humans over time to become useful.

hibernate
To spend winter asleep.

malaria
A disease passed on by mosquitos.

nectar
A sweet liquid secreted by some flowers.

nymph
The water-living stage of some insects' lives.

ornamental
Attractive to look at.

predators
Animals that hunt other animals for food.

prey
An animal that is hunted for food.

temperate
An area with mild temperatures.

tropical
A hot and humid climate.

Index